LIGHTNING BOLT BOOKS™

The Capitol Building

Janet Piehl

Lerner Publications Company
Minneapolis

For my
Schmidt relatives,
who first showed
me the Capitol

Lerner Publications Company
A division of Lerner Publishing Group, Inc.
241 First Avenue North
Minneapolis, MN 55401 U.S.A.

Website address: www.lernerbooks.com

Library of Congress Cataloging-in-Publication Data

Piehl, Janet.
    The Capitol Building / by Janet Piehl.
        p.   cm. — (Lightning bolt books™—famous places)
    Includes index.
    ISBN 978–1–57505–966–2 (lib. bdg. : alk. paper)
    1. United States Capitol (Washington, D.C.)—Juvenile literature. 2. Washington (D.C.)—Buildings,
structures, etc.—Juvenile literature. I. Title.
    F204.C2P54 2010
    975.3—dc22   2008047174

Manufactured in the United States of America
1 2 3 4 5 6 — BP — 15 14 13 12 11 10

Contents

What Is the Capitol? **page 5**

Building the Capitol **page 10**

A Visit to the Capitol **page 20**

Map **page 28**

Fun Facts **page 29**

Glossary **page 30**

Further Reading **page 31**

Index **page 32**

What is the Capitol?

Have you ever seen this building? **It is the Capitol of the United States.**

The U.S. Capitol is a large, white building. It sits on top of a hill.

The Capitol is where our country's laws are made. Congress meets in the Capitol to make those laws.

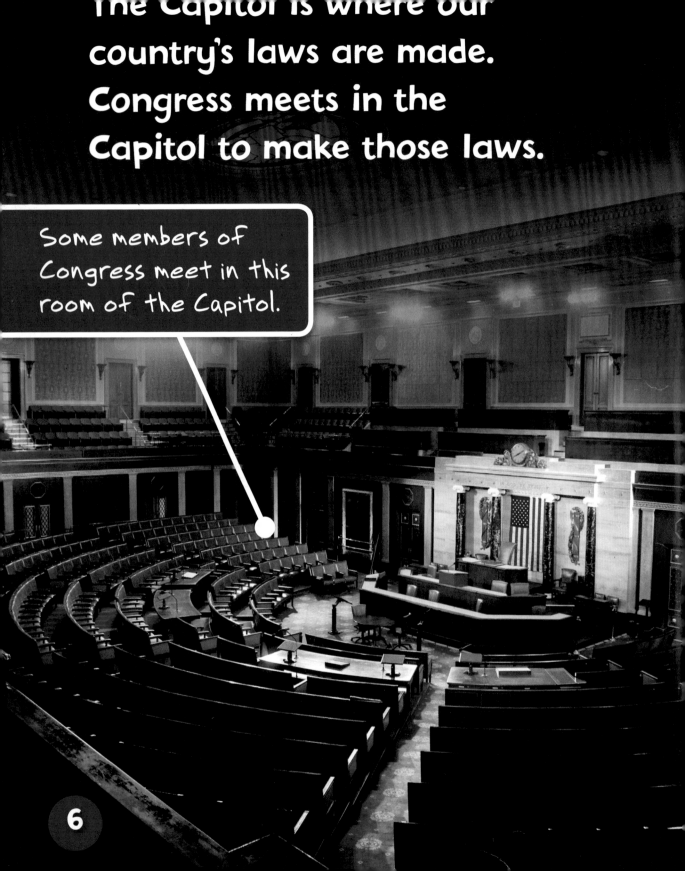

Some members of Congress meet in this room of the Capitol.

The Senate and the House of Representatives make up Congress.

Senators meet in the Senate chamber. Visitors can sit in the upper level.

The **Capitol** is in Washington, D.C. Washington is the capital city of the United States. Government leaders make important decisions there.

The president and vice president talk about important issues with other government leaders.

The Capitol sits high on Capitol Hill. You can see it from all over Washington.

Here's the Capitol!

Building the Capitol

The United States was a new country in the 1790s. Its new Congress needed a place to meet. The government held a contest to choose a design for this meeting place. Dr. William Thornton won the contest in 1792. His design was used to build the Capitol.

Dr. William Thornton

Thornton drew this picture of what he thought the country's capitol should look like.

The design showed two wings. They were connected by a dome.

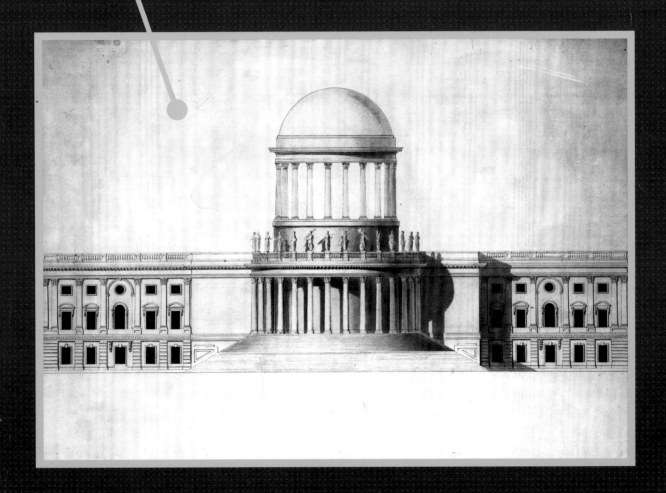

Building began in 1793.
Workers used sandstone
to build the Capitol.
Sandstone is a type of rock.

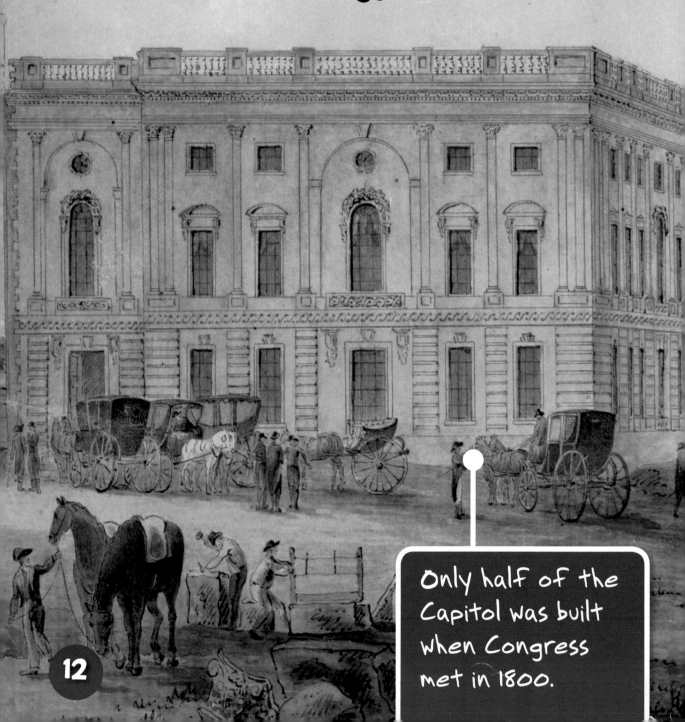

Only half of the
Capitol was built
when Congress
met in 1800.

By 1800, only the north wing had been finished.

But Congress met there anyway.

The **Capitol** had two wings by 1811. They were both shaped like rectangles.

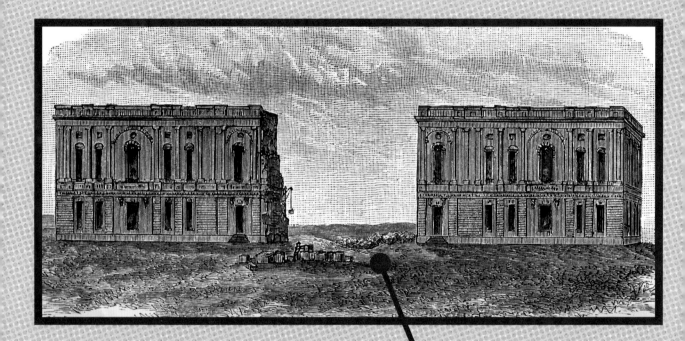

A wooden passage would connect the two wings.

The Capitol looked like this before a wooden passage was built between the two wings.

British soldiers invaded Washington in 1814. They set fire to the Capitol. The building was in ruins.

Workers had to rebuild the Capitol. They added a round room. It is called the Rotunda. It connects the two wings.

Workers built a dome over the Rotunda.

The dome was made of wood. It was covered with copper.

The United States was growing fast. New states joined the nation. The new states sent new members to Congress. The Congress needed more space in the Capitol. Larger wings were built in the 1850s. They were made of marble.

The new wings made the Capitol twice as long as it had been.

The Capitol needed a bigger dome too. Workers finished the new dome in 1863. It was made of cast iron. The new dome weighed almost 9 million pounds (4 million kilograms)!

The new dome is nearly complete in this picture from 1863.

A bronze statue of a woman stands on top of the dome. The statue is called *Freedom*. It is 19.5 feet (6 meters) tall.

The statue Freedom faces east.

A Visit to the Capitol

Did you know that you can visit the Capitol? You can see where Congress meets. The Senate meets in the north wing. The House of Representatives meets in the south wing.

The Capitol as seen from above

Visitors to the U.S. Capitol Visitor Center can see a model of the statue *Freedom*. The visitor center opened in 2008.

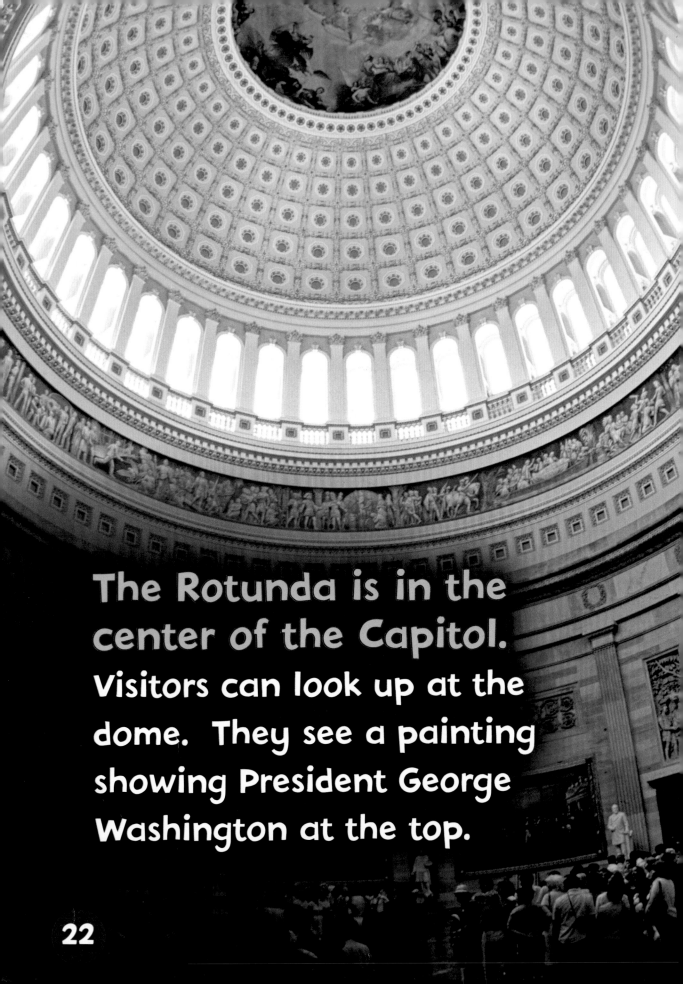

The Rotunda is in the center of the Capitol. Visitors can look up at the dome. They see a painting showing President George Washington at the top.

Visitors can see statues of famous Americans at the Capitol. Many of them are in National Statuary Hall.

The House of Representatives met in Statuary Hall until 1857. The hall is shaped like a half circle. It holds thirty-eight statues.

The President's Room is one of the grandest parts of the Capitol. Senators use the room most often.

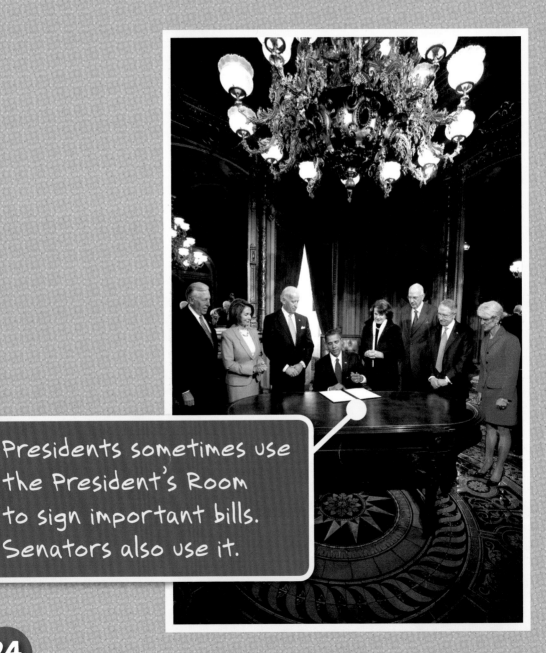

Presidents sometimes use the President's Room to sign important bills. Senators also use it.

Some members of Congress have offices in the Capitol. Some have offices nearby. The Capitol is part of a group of buildings called the Capitol Complex.

The Capitol Complex includes the Capitol (center), four offices for the House of Representatives (left), and two Senate office buildings (right).

Underground tunnels and a subway connect the office buildings to the Capitol.

Subway cars help people travel quickly from building to building in the Capitol Complex.

Presidents take the oath of office on the steps of the Capitol. The world watches the Capitol. It is a symbol of the United States and its government. The Capitol is one of the most important buildings in the world.

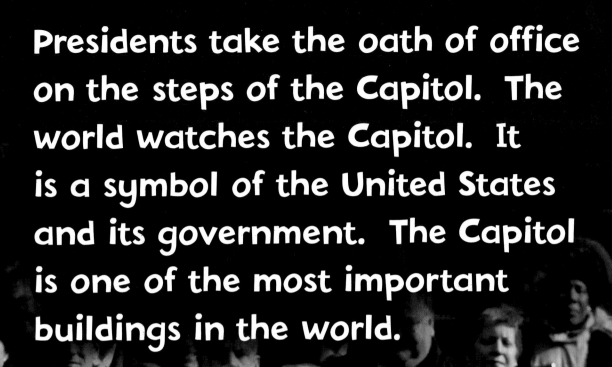

President Barack Obama took the oath of office in January 2009.

Washington, D.C., Area

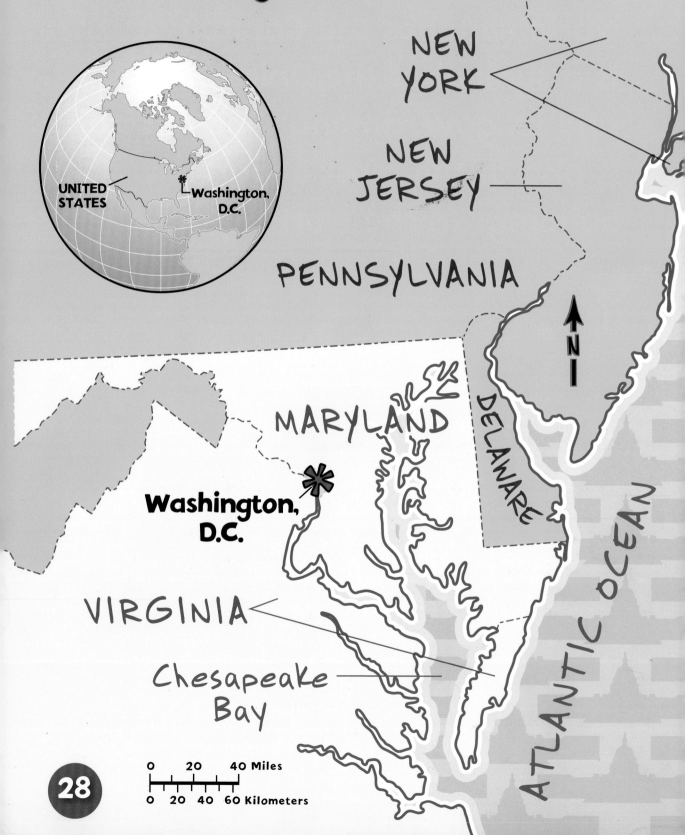

NEW YORK

NEW JERSEY

PENNSYLVANIA

UNITED STATES

Washington, D.C.

MARYLAND

DELAWARE

N

Washington, D.C.

VIRGINIA

Chesapeake Bay

ATLANTIC OCEAN

0   20   40 Miles

0   20   40   60 Kilometers

Fun Facts

- President George Washington laid the Capitol's cornerstone, or first stone, in 1793.

- The Capitol is about 751 feet (229 m) long, from north to south. That means it is about as long as two-and-a-half football fields.

- There are 540 rooms, 658 windows, and 850 doorways in the Capitol.

- Visitors can tell when Congress is meeting without going into the Capitol. A lantern on top of the dome shines when Congress is in session. A flag flies over the north wing when the Senate is at work. A flag flies over the south wing when the House of Representatives meets.

- The U.S. Capitol Visitor Center opened to the public on December 2, 2008. Here, visitors can learn more about the Capitol and Congress and arrange for tours.

Glossary

capital city: a city where a government is based. Washington, D.C., is the capital city of the United States.

Capitol: the building where U.S. Congress meets to make laws

cast iron: a strong, hard metal made in a mold, or cast

Congress: the part of the U.S. government that makes laws. Congress is made up of two parts—the Senate and the House of Representatives.

House of Representatives: part of Congress. The House of Representatives has 435 members. People from each state elect representatives.

Rotunda: a round room in the Capitol. The Rotunda is covered by a dome.

Senate: part of Congress. The Senate has 100 members. People from each state elect two people to the Senate.

symbol: something that stands for something else. The Capitol is a symbol of the United States and its government.

wing: a part of a building. Wings usually stick out from the main part of a building. The Capitol has two wings that connect to a dome.

Further Reading

Ben's Guide to U.S. Government for Kids
http://bensguide.gpo.gov/3-5/symbols/capitol.html

Kids in the House: The Office of the Clerk
http://clerkkids.house.gov/index.html

Kishel, Ann-Marie. *U.S. Symbols.* Minneapolis: Lerner Publications Company, 2007.

Murray, Julie. *White House.* Edina, MN: Abdo, 2003.

Silate, Jennifer. *The United States Capitol.* New York: PowerKids Press, 2006.

The United States Capitol Historical Society Presents: A Tour of the Capitol
http://uschscapitolhistory.uschs.org/tour/01_b.htm

Index

burning of the Capitol, 15

Congress, 6–7, 10, 12, 17, 20, 25, 29

design, 10–11
dome, 16, 18–19

Freedom, 19, 21

House of Representatives, 7, 20, 23, 25, 29

National Statuary Hall, 23

president, 8, 22, 24, 27
President's Room, 24

Rotunda, 16, 22

Senate, 7, 20, 25, 29
Senate chamber, 7

Visitor Center, 21, 29

Washington, D.C., 8–9, 15, 28
Washington, George, 22, 29
wings, 11–12, 14, 16–17, 20

Photo Acknowledgments

The images in this book are used with the permission of: © EyeWire/Getty Images, pp. 2, 4; © Marc Muench/Stone/Getty Images, p. 5; © Brendan Hoffman/Getty Images, p. 6; AP Photo/U.S. Senate, p. 7; AP Photo/J. Scott Applewhite, p. 8; © Sissie Brimberg/National Geographic/Getty Images, p. 9; © Smithsonian American Art Museum, Washington, D.C./ Art Resource, NY, p. 10; Library of Congress, pp. 11 (LC-USZC4-113), 12–13 (LC-USZC4-247), 18 (LC-DIG-ppmsca-07302); © North Wind Picture Archives, p. 14; © Bettmann/CORBIS, p. 15; AP Photo/John Plumbe Jr., p. 16; The Granger Collection, New York, p. 17; © Glowimages/ Getty Images, p. 19; © H. Armstrong Roberts/Retrofile/Getty Images, p. 20; AP Photo/Jacquelyn Martin, p. 21; © Kenneth Garrett/National Geographic/Getty Images, p. 22; © Kurt Scholz/ SuperStock, p. 23; © Molly Riley/AFP/Getty Images, p. 24; © Randy Santos/SuperStock, p. 25; Architect of the Capitol, p. 26; © Alex Wong/Getty Images, p. 27; © Laura Westlund/Independent Picture Service, p. 28; © Travelpix Ltd/Photographer's Choice/Getty Images, p. 31.

Front Cover: © Travelpix Ltd/Photographer's Choice/Getty Images.